LEVEL 6

Written by: Caroline Laidlaw
Series Editor: Melanie Williams

Pearson Education Limited
Edinburgh Gate, Harlow,
Essex CM20 2JE, England
and Associated Companies throughout the world.

ISBN: 978-1-4082-8848-1

This edition first published by Pearson Education Ltd 2013
9 10 8
Text copyright © Pearson Education Ltd 2013

The moral rights of the author have been asserted
in accordance with the Copyright Designs and Patents Act 1988

Set in 15/19pt OT Fiendstar
Printed in China
SWTC/08

Acknowledgements

The publisher would like to thank the following for their kind permission to reproduce their photographs:
(Key: b-bottom; c-centre; l-left; r-right; t-top)

Alamy Images: Chris Mattison 19b, Chris Wildblood 22t, chrisstockphoto 22b, E.R. Degginger 3cl, 7t, Kevin Schafer 40 (5), Konstantin Bordukov 40 (3), MShieldsPhotos 40 (2); **Ardea:** Alan Weaving 27t, Pat Morris 37tr; **Corbis:** David A. Northcott 19t, Flip Nicklin / Minden Pictures 5, Gary Meszaros / Visuals Unlimited 3r, 34t, Gary W. Carter 11, Nigel J. Dennis / Gallo Images 16-17, Tom Brakefield 29b, Wim van Egmond / Visuals Unlimited 36; **DK Images:** Jerry Young 32t; **FLPA Images of Nature:** Birgitte Wilms / Minden Pictures 35b, Cyril Ruoso / Minden Pictures 13t, Donald M. Jones / Minden Pictures 30c, ImageBroker 17 (inset), Michael & Patricia Fogden / Minden Pictures 23, Neil Bowman 21, Piotr Naskrecki / Minden Pictures 14t, 27 (inset), 27b, Rolf Nussbaumer / Imagebroker 8t, Yva Momatiuk & John Eastcott / Minden Pictures 25; **Fotolia.com:** 30t, 35t; **Getty Images:** Borat Furlan 26b, David Barcroft 28, Flickr 14b, Gail Shumway 3cr, 30b, Michael & Patricia Fogden 12-13, Visuals Unlimited, Inc. / Leroy Simon 10; **RNDr. Jan Sevcik:** 19c; **Masterfile UK Ltd:** Noel Hendrickson 9br; **Nature Picture Library:** Brandon Cole 6b, George McCarthy 31 (inset bottom), James Brickell 32b, Markus Varesvuo 31 (inset top), Nature Production 3l, 9t, Nick Garbutt 20, Patricio Robles Gil 9bl, Peter Blackwell 18, Peter Scoones 6t, Robert Valentic 33b, Stephen Dalton 11 (inset), 14 (inset), Tom Vezo 31, Wild Wonders of Europe / Geslin 15; **Rex Features:** Andrew Stewart / SpecialistStock 29t; **Shutterstock.com:** 7b, 13b, 34c, 34b, 40 (4), ittipon 8b; **SuperStock:** 24, imagebroker.net 33t, Minden Pictures 40 (1), Prisma 26t, Science Faction 37tl

Cover images: *Front:* **Alamy Images:** Chris Mattison

All other images © Pearson Education

In some instances we have been unable to trace the owners of copyright material,
and we would appreciate any information that would enable us to do so.

Illustrations: Jackie Stafford

All rights reserved; no part of this publication may be reproduced, stored in a retrieval system,
or transmitted in any form or by any means, electronic, mechanical, photocopying,
recording or otherwise, without the prior written permission of the Publishers.

For a complete list of the titles available in the Pearson English Kids Readers series, please go to
www.pearsonenglishkidsreaders.com. Alternatively, write to your local Pearson Education office or to
Pearson English Readers Marketing Department, Pearson Education, Edinburgh Gate, Harlow, Essex CM202JE, England.

Contents

Hiding from Danger	4
Disguises in the Sea	6
Hiding on Plants	8
Hiding on the Ground	12
Hiding in Trees	19
Stripes and Spots	24
Fur and Feathers	28
Is it Real or is it a Copy?	32
The Best Tricks and Disguises	35
Glossary	38
Activities	39

Hiding from Danger

Hello! I'm Marko, the Octopus. The shark was a hungry predator and it could swim fast. So, how did I escape? I just climbed onto a rock and disguised myself. I couldn't swim fast enough to escape. The fish didn't see me because I disappeared. I'm good at tricks. An octopus can change colour to match the colour of the rock. Now I am the same colour as I was before.

When animals hide themselves in this way, it is called camouflage. Sometimes predators hide when they are hunting. Other animals hide because they are a meal for predators. We call a hunted animal prey.

There's more than one way to escape a predator, you know. Can you see a fish in this picture? It is almost invisible, isn't it? Its body is always the same colour as the sand. This fish cannot change colour to escape. It must stay quietly in the surroundings which match its colour. If it moves, a predator will see it.

This kind of camouflage can protect the fish because it is a disguise which works well.

Disguises in the Sea

This seahorse has one of the best disguises in the ocean. Where did the leaves come from? They are part of the seahorse's body. A predator may see the leaves, but not the seahorse. It is a great way to avoid danger.

Another seahorse lives in more colourful surroundings where it needs a different disguise. Can you see the seahorse in the pink and white coral? Its body looks like real coral.

coral

seahorse

Did you know? Before baby seahorses are born, they grow inside their father's body. No other male animal can do this.

Balloon fish

A Balloon fish can change its shape when it is in danger. Its yellow and white body has black spots, and spikes which lie against the fish's body. When the fish sees a predator, it fills itself with water or air to look much bigger. The spikes round its body stand up and look hard and sharp.

Wise predators will not attack a spiky ball. They are stupid if they try. Why? The spikes can hurt a predator's mouth. Even worse, the fish itself is poisonous, and can kill. This clever disguise protects both the Balloon fish and its predator.

Hiding on Plants

What has six legs, a head, a body and often one or two pairs of wings? The answer is an insect. No-one knows how many different kinds of insect there are. Scientists are discovering new ones all the time because they are very good at hiding.

Insects are everywhere, and in every habitat on earth. They even live in the fur on animals' bodies. Many insects camouflage themselves to match their surroundings.

This green mantis is almost invisible on leaves. It waits for other insects which are its prey. Only the best detective can avoid this ambush.

mantis

The body of this mantis is a different colour because it lives on flowers. Do you think it matches the flower's colour exactly? Not really. We can still see it but that does not matter. We are not mantis prey.

There are a lot of insects which live on plants. Not all of them are predators. Stick insects, for example, only eat leaves. Their long thin bodies look like sticks. If they want to escape their predators, they must sit quietly on a leaf.

Did you know?
In some countries stick insects are pets. In other countries people eat them.

caterpillar

Do you sometimes wear a disguise, maybe for a party? Would you like to be an actor and wear different clothes? Well, there is a caterpillar which likes acting and wearing something different. It is not really an actor, of course. It just wants to avoid the eyes of greedy birds. It camouflages itself with bits of flowers which it attaches to its body.

What happens if the caterpillar eats all the pink flowers, or just gets bored? The answer is easy. It can move to a flower with a different colour, and change the clothes on its back.

Spiders are not insects because they have eight legs, but they do like eating insects. A good place to ambush prey is on flowers. Insects often visit flowers where they can get a sweet drink. Small Crab spiders sit in their pretty surroundings and wait for food. Prey insects only notice these spiders if they move.

Crab spider

Can a yellow Crab spider move to a white flower? Yes it can, but it could be hungry for a few weeks afterwards. It can take a month or more before its body changes colour. Then it will match the white flower.

Hiding on the Ground

The Sleepy lizard lives in Australia, in dry habitats. How many heads has this brown lizard got? Only one real head but its tail could be a head, too. A predator will make a mistake if it attacks the wrong end. Then the lizard will drop its tail and escape. It leaves behind a tasty snack for the predator. A new tail will grow again in about a year's time.

Sleepy lizards would prefer to keep their tails, if possible. They try frightening the predator first. They show their teeth, make a horrible noise and bite.

Sleepy lizards match their surroundings. They can be dark or light brown, or grey with white or yellow markings. They find plant food, insects and small animals on the ground where they live.

Sleepy lizard

Another kind of Australian lizard, the Spiky lizard, has yellow, orange, brown and white markings, and sharp spikes on its body. This camouflage protects it in the driest habitats of Australia, where it is sandy and usually terribly hot. It is a hard place to live.

Spiky lizard

ants

Did you know?
A Spiky lizard only eats ants.
It can eat 1,000 in one meal.

Ants are prey for lizards and other animals, but they are also predators. There are hundreds of different kinds of ants. They live together in nests, which are often under the ground. Ants' nests may also be inside walls of buildings or in trees and in other places. A lot of ants are the same colour as the ground where they move. It is often difficult to see them when they are hurrying here and there.

The insect in the picture is not an ant, but it uses black ants to disguise itself. How? After it kills some ants, it eats a few. Then it attaches some dead ants' bodies to its back and runs off.

If a hungry Wolf spider notices this strange disguise, the insect is in big trouble. Wolf spiders have excellent eyes, and are always watching out for a meal.

They live in holes in the ground, where they quietly sit and hide. They are usually brown, black, and grey, and not bright and colourful. Some of them have stripes and other markings. Their prey will probably not notice these hunting spiders in their surroundings.

Wolf spider

Meerkats live in the Kalahari Desert and other parts of Southern Africa. Their fur is usually light brown with grey markings, and they also have camouflage stripes across their backs.

Meerkats work in teams. There are always a few watching out for enemies in the sky and on the ground. Big birds hunt them from above, and wild dogs, cats and snakes also try to catch them. Meerkats are brave animals when a predator comes too near. They will lie together on their backs, and show their sharp teeth. They look like one big, fierce animal which is very frightening.

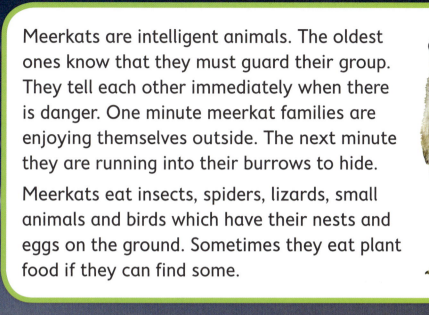

Meerkats are intelligent animals. The oldest ones know that they must guard their group. They tell each other immediately when there is danger. One minute meerkat families are enjoying themselves outside. The next minute they are running into their burrows to hide.

Meerkats eat insects, spiders, lizards, small animals and birds which have their nests and eggs on the ground. Sometimes they eat plant food if they can find some.

meerkat

Did you know?
As many as forty meerkats live in one group. All the meerkats in a group go to the same place when they need a toilet.

Lions are big predators. Some of them live in Asia, but most lions live in Africa. Their bodies are a light yellow-brown colour to match the colours of hot, open grassland. They are a darker colour in habitats where there are more plants and trees.

In the grasslands of the Serengeti in Tanzania, a lion's coat is a perfect camouflage. The big cat will lie quietly in the grass, and jump out to surprise its prey.

Lions work together in a team when they hunt. They prefer catching big animals, because these can feed all the lions in the family.

Hiding in Trees

Tree snakes spend a lot of time living and hunting in trees. They are long, thin and good at climbing. The colour of their bodies matches their surroundings. They sometimes come down from trees to hunt on the ground. They catch frogs, lizards and birds. This Tree snake is finishing a big meal.

A Tree frog is almost invisible on a green leaf. The top of its body is bright green. It has amazing feet which can hold on to leaves when it jumps.

Geckos are colourful lizards which live in rainforests, deserts and mountains. Most geckos hunt at night, so they have to hide from their enemies in the day. A few are busy during the day when they look for insects, fruits and sweet juice in flowers.

In Madagascar the rainforests are full of geckos, but they are usually invisible. Many of them look like part of the tree which they are resting on. Some of them look like dead leaves on the ground. The markings and colours of their camouflaged bodies make geckos hard to see in the forest.

gecko

Geckos often live around people's homes. They climb and run across ceilings and up and down walls. People like them in their houses because they eat biting insects.

Geckos are not the same as other lizards because they have voices. They can make a noise which frightens their enemies. Their name 'gecko' sounds like this noise. Some geckos protect themselves in another way, too. They make a horrible smell when a snake or bird attacks them. Anything is better than that smell, so the predator quickly goes away.

Did you know?
In Southeast Asia some people say geckos bring good luck.

In Namibia there is a very small owl which hides against a tree during the day. Its feathers are brown and grey, and it is almost invisible.

The owl has big, bright orange eyes. These help it to see when it is looking for food at night. In the day time the owl must keep its eyes shut. If the owl opens them, a predator will notice its bright eyes and kill it.

Sloths live in the rainforests of Central and South America. They spend their lives in trees, and only come down about once a week. They find a place for a toilet on the ground, then they climb up another tree.

Everything a sloth does is slow. It eats slowly, moves slowly and sleeps most of the time.

There is something strange about a sloth's fur, because it looks green. It is covered with small green plants called algae. This is excellent camouflage in leafy trees. Not many predators notice an animal which almost never moves.

sloth

Stripes and Spots

The tiger is one of the most endangered animals on earth. Once there were nine different kinds of tiger in Asia. Now three of these are extinct. Why? Do the camouflage stripes on its body fail to protect it? Camouflage does hide tigers from their prey, but not from people who kill them.

The other problem is tigers' habitats, which are getting smaller every year.

Zebras also have stripes, but they are not endangered. They are a kind of horse, with black and white stripes. They live in Africa where their predators are lions and wild dogs.

Black and white stripes are easy to see, so how can these markings protect a zebra? They do not match the surroundings, do they? That is true if it is people who are looking. Our eyes see colour but a lion's eyes cannot see colour. They only see black and white stripy grass and stripy zebras.

When a crowd of zebras is on grassland, predators cannot see a single zebra. They just see a lot of stripes.

Did you know? Not all zebras sleep at night. Some are awake to guard the group, because many predators hunt at night.

zebra

There are fish in the ocean which do exactly the same thing as zebras. They move in a crowd, because the sea can be a very dangerous place.

A predator sees a single fish more clearly when it is swimming alone. When a big crowd of fish swims past, it may look like one big, strange animal. A crowd of stripy fish looks stranger.

Fish also use spots to protect themselves. A single spot near a fish's tail looks like an eye, which could be a surprise for predators. The fish in the picture is a Butterfly fish.

Spots on a butterfly's wings do not really look like eyes. They are bright markings which may frighten a bird or insect. The butterfly in the picture has wings with red and blue spots.

Much more surprising are the spots which a katydid hides. This insect looks like a dead leaf on the ground. If a gecko, spider or frog goes towards it, the katydid opens its wings to show a pair of bright spots. This is usually enough to frighten most hunting animals. First they see an old dead leaf. Then suddenly they discover something alive.

katydids

Fur and Feathers

In the Arctic, snow and ice cover the ground for much of the year. The Arctic wolf's thick white fur is perfect for this habitat. It keeps it warm and also hides the wolf from prey. The wolf uses its tail to cover its nose and mouth when it sleeps.

The Arctic wolf has few predators. These are grey wolves, wild dogs and polar bears. In the short summer between June and August, small plants grow. Animals and birds find more to eat then, but they themselves may become food for the wolf.

Arctic wolf

Polar bear

Harp seal

Polar bears live in an Arctic habitat, too. Their thick white coats make them almost invisible.

Harp seals often swim under the Arctic ice. They cannot breathe under water so they come up for air. This is a dangerous time if the seals do not see a waiting Polar bear. Baby Harp seals are in greater danger, because they move slowly. Their parents hope their babies are safe. Why? Because baby Harp seals are born with white fur.

The world's climate is changing, so there is less Arctic ice. It is getting more difficult for Polar bears to hunt seals.

Snowy owls live in the icy world of the Arctic. Their white camouflaged feathers protect them when they hunt in both light and dark. Most other owls only hunt at night.

The owls build nests on the ground, and carefully guard their eggs and young family. They will even attack a wolf which comes near the nest.

Snowshoe hares live in the north of North America. The colour of their fur changes with the seasons. In summer they are brown and in winter they are white. Snowshoe hares are larger than rabbits. Predators are owls, wolves, people and other animals.

Snowshoe hares

The Willow ptarmigan also lives in colder parts of North America. Its feathers change colour from light brown in summer to snowy white in winter. In all seasons, the bird's camouflage matches its surroundings. When the female bird is on her nest, she is almost invisible.

In winter, Willow ptarmigans make burrows in the snow to stay warm. They fly straight into the deep snow. If they walk, predators might see their tracks in the snow. Then the predators could find the Willow ptarmigans in their burrows.

Willow ptarmigan

Did you know?
The Willow ptarmigan's eggs look like real stones.

Is it Real or is it a Copy?

There are animals which look like sticks, green leaves or dead leaves. The Asian Dead Leaf frog in the picture is hard to see because it does not look like a frog. Its brown body copies the colour and shape of dead leaves. Lizards and snakes eat frogs, but not this one. They will notice it only if it moves.

Look at the brown leaves in the picture below. Small animals and birds should keep clear. A venomous snake is hiding and waiting for them. One bite will kill its prey.

Coral snake

Brightly coloured snakes are usually venomous. Their colour tells predators, 'If you come near me you'll be sorry!' For this reason, some snakes have colours and markings which copy dangerous snakes.

There are two snakes in North America which look almost the same. The Milk snake is not dangerous, but the Coral snake is venomous. Do predators attack both these snakes? They must be careful, because they might make a mistake. They might attack the wrong one, which could kill them.

Milk snake

Did you know?
People also kill Milk snakes, because they look venomous. This camouflage does not always work well.

Caterpillars are not big animals. They have to be small if they are going to move around leaves and eat them. Could a caterpillar ever look like a snake? Look at the picture. Is it a snake or is it a caterpillar? A predator does not wait to find out. It just gets away fast.

Most predators avoid eating Monarch butterflies because they taste horrible. The Viceroy butterfly is clever to look like the Monarch. A bird may notice it, but would prefer not to make a mistake. The Viceroy butterfly copies the Monarch's colours and markings to protect itself.

Viceroy butterfly

Monarch butterfly

The Best Tricks and Disguises?

Animals in the sea have some of the best disguises. Two clever crabs have different ways of hiding from prey to avoid predators.

One good trick is to live in an empty seashell. Not many crab predators can break it. If you have a soft body, the hard seashell protects you. It is also easy to move into another seashell when you grow bigger.

Another clever trick is to attach small plants and animals to your back. Then you can be almost invisible on the floor of the ocean.

I don't want to sound clever, but octopuses really do have the best disguises. First, we can change colour. You already know that.

We can also change shape. You didn't know that, did you? We can copy a venomous Sea snake with black and white stripes. We can look like a Lion fish, with its poisonous spikes.

And my very best trick? I can shoot a cloud of black ink into the water when a predator is following me. I just disappear. Wait a minute. Here comes a shark. I'll show you!

Glossary

algae (n) page 23   a very small plant which lives in wet places, or on water

camouflage (n) page 5   colour, markings, and sometimes the shape of an animal's body, which matches the animal's surroundings; camouflage helps an animal to hide from its enemies

crab (n) page 35

desert (n) page 16   a dry habitat which gets little or no rain

disguise (n and v) page 4   the way an animal looks when it wants to look like something else

habitat (n) page 8   the place where an animal usually lives

invisible (adj) page 5   an invisible thing is something which you cannot see

octopus (n) page 4

predator (n) page 4   an animal which hunts other animals for food

prey (n) page 5   an animal which is food for other animals

Activity page 1

Before You Read

1 Look at the cover. What is this book about?
Answer 'Yes', 'No' or 'Maybe'.

   a Animals which live in zoos.
   b Animals which sometimes hide from other animals.
   c Places where animals might hide.
   d Animals which work with people on farms.
   e Animals which are extinct.
   f Animals which scientists study.

2 Where do the animals live? Match the animals with the places (habitats). Some animals live in more than one habitat.

   a in the sea
   b in grasslands and fields
   c in rainforests
   d in people's gardens and homes
   e in rivers and lakes

39

Activity page 2

After You Read

1 Match the animals with the descriptions.

1 A seahorse is
2 A stick insect sits
3 Meerkats are
4 A gecko is
5 Snowy owls are
6 An octopus has

a Small animals with light brown and grey markings. They live in family groups.
b many disguises.
c a small animal which hides itself in sea plants or coral.
d large white birds.
e on a plant and looks like a stick.
f a kind of lizard which is good at disguising itself in trees.

2 Look at the animal disguises and complete the sentences.

1 The mantis looks like a _____
2 The insect looks like a _____
3 The willow ptarmigan's eggs look like _____
4 The balloon fish looks like a _____
5 The spider looks like a _____